Warriors and Wenches

D0452871

For Jeremy, Lola and Madison

Warriors and Wenches

Michelle Rosenberg

PEN & SWORD HISTORY

AN IMPRINT OF PEN & SWORD BOOKS LTD.
YORKSHIRE – PHILADELPHIA

First published in Great Britain in 2019 by
PEN AND SWORD HISTORY
an imprint of
Pen & Sword Books Ltd
Yorkshire – Philadelphia

Copyright © Michelle Rosenberg, 2019

ISBN 978 1 47389 936 0

Printed and bound in the UK by TJ International Ltd,
Padstow, Cornwall

Typeset in Times New Roman by
Aura Technology and Software Services, India

Pen & Sword Books Ltd incorporates the imprints of Pen & Sword
Archaeology, Atlas, Aviation, Battleground, Discovery,
Family History, History, Maritime, Military, Naval, Politics, Railways,
Select, Social History, Transport, True Crime, Claymore Press,
Frontline Books, Leo Cooper, Praetorian Press, Remember When,
Seaforth Publishing and Wharncliffe.

For a complete list of Pen & Sword titles please contact
PEN & SWORD BOOKS LIMITED
47 Church Street, Barnsley, South Yorkshire, S70 2AS, England
E-mail: enquiries@pen-and-sword.co.uk
Website: www.pen-and-sword.co.uk

Or
PEN AND SWORD BOOKS
1950 Lawrence Rd, Havertown, PA 19083, USA
E-mail: Uspen-and-sword@casematepublishers.com
Website: www.penandswordbooks.com

Contents

Introduction 7

WARRIORS

Penthesilea, Queen of the Amazons 10

Artemisia of Caria (aka Artemisia I) 13

Boudicca/Boadicea (died c. AD 60/61) 16

Khutulun (1260-1306) 20

Joan of Arc (c. 1412-30 May 1431) 22

Caterina Sforza (1463-28 May 1509) aka the Lioness
    of the Romagna, Lady of Imola, Countess of Forli 25

Grace O'Malley (1530-1603) Gráinne Ní Mháille, aka
    Grace O'Malley, Queen of Umail and the Pirate
    Queen of Ireland 28

Catalina de Erauso (1585/92-1650) aka the Lieutenant Nun 31

Ulricka Eleonora Stålhammar (c.1688-16 February 1733).......... 34

Nakano Takeko - (1846/47-1868) 37

Mariya Oktyabrskaya (16 August 1905-15 March 1944) 39

Susan Travers (23 September 1909-18 December 2003)............. 41

Lyudmila Pavlichenko (1916-10 October 1974).......................... 43

Faye Schulman (November 28, 1919 -)..................................... 46

Hannah Szenes (Senesh) (17 July 1921-7 November 1944)........ 48

WENCHES

Phryne the Thespian (c 371-310 BC)...52

Alice Perrers aka Alice de Windsor (1348-1400) 55

Imperia Cognati, the First Courtesan
    (3 August 1486-15 August 1512) 58

Diane de Poitiers
    (3 September 1499-25 April 1566)..61

Mary Boleyn (1499/1500-19 July 1543)......................................64

Veronica Franco (1546–1591)..68

Barbara Palmer, nee Villiers, Duchess of Cleveland,
    Countess of Castlemaine (17 November 1640-1709)...............71

Nell Gwynne (2 February 1650-14 November 1687).......................75

Kate Hackabout (b. Unknown-based on Hogarth's
    painting, 2 September 1731)...78

Madame/Marquise de Pompadour
    (c. December 1721-15 April 1764)..81

Madame du Barry (19 August 1743-8 December 1793) 85

Grace Dalrymple (c. 1754-1823)..88

Harriette Wilson (22 February 1786-10 March 1845).................91

Esther Lachmann aka La Païva (1819-84)...................................95

La Barucci (Giulia Beneni) 1837[?]-70/1)...................................98

Introduction

'When the destiny of a nation is in a woman's bedroom,
the best place for the historian is in the antechamber.'
Charles-Augustin Sainte-Reuve

Until relatively recently, history books and traditional school lessons have focused on the same few women, held up as examples of female achievement. On the positive side, times are changing. Women's history has become more prevalent in our collective consciousness, whether in the news, in books, through commemorative events like International Women's Day, the #MeToo movement, charities, education and through writers and academics.

There are countless women whose stories should be told. *Warriors and Wenches* highlights the fact that world history is full of women we don't know about.

Those women we do know about are often recorded, not specifically because of achievements in their own right, but because of their relation to a particular man in history. They are a wife, a mistress, a mother – as opposed to themselves. For others, their stories have been overlooked or airbrushed from history. And for those whose names we will never know – their number is incalculable. Historically, career and life choices for women have been limited and women's lives weren't deemed important enough to record.

Warriors and Wenches showcases just some of those who took matters into their own hands, lived their lives on their own terms and were forces to reckon with.

The 'wenches' would have been called tarts, whores, courtesans, mistresses or prostitutes. The 'warriors' often had to disguise their sex in order to fight. These are women you should know about.

Love them or loathe them, they made their mark and were often so extraordinary that their lives were recorded at times when women's stories traditionally weren't.

Warriors and Wenches offers up an indulgent romp through centuries of history, featuring women who cross dressed as soldiers, widows turned tank drivers bent on bloody vengeance and fierce martial arts fighters to women who magnificently and outrageously schemed to turn their social lot in life to their advantage: the mistresses, courtesans and uniquely French maitresse-en-titres who wielded incredible power and influence in the sumptuous courts of Europe.

This book doesn't seek to decide whether these women were 'good' or 'bad'; I will leave it up to you to make up your own minds. These are women who, through military skill, incredible courage and loyalty, scandal, poison plots and sexual debauchery, have crossed over into the realm of legend and myth and become powerful symbols of feminist power.

Michelle Rosenberg

WARRIORS

Penthesilea, Queen of the Amazons

Amazons: the legendary tribe of women warriors, led by their Queen Hippolyte, now front and centre in the public eye following the smash hit *Wonder Woman* with the awesome butt-kicking Gal Gadot. These Scythian warriors are the stuff of legend. Mythical, marvellous, badass, and the equals of men in every way.

Members of this ultimate matriarchal society allegedly cut off one breast in order to make them better archers with their bow. Or of course that could have simply been propaganda of their enemies, the Greeks. You were only a true Greek hero if you conquered, fought or defeated an Amazonian warrior.

An archaeological discovery on the Russian border with Kazakhstan revealed over 150 graves or kurgans, burial mounds of a nomadic people the Greeks referred to as Scythians. They prove that there were indeed warrior women that fit the description of the Amazons. Whatever their men did, they did. They rode horses, they were very tall for their time, they had tattoos, fought, hunted for food. They were also buried with hemp-making kits and tattoo kits. If they gave birth to sons, the boys would be left with other tribes for fostering and as a way of cementing good inter-tribal relationships.

Legend and myth has it that Penthesilea, the daughter of Ares, the Greek God of War, and Otrera was the mythological Queen of the Amazons of Asia Minor during the Trojan War.

Roman historian Pliny claims that Penthesilea was beautiful and wise, highly skilled in weaponry and a fierce warrior and that she invented the battle axe. Her story is told in the lost Greek literary epic *Aethiopis*, of which only five lines survive.

Her tale is tempered by tragedy. Whilst out hunting she accidentally killed her sister Hippolyte with (depending on the story you read) either an arrow or a spear. Consumed by grief and regret, she wanted only to die, but as a warrior could only do so honourably in battle.

The great warrior Achilles supports the slumping figure of the Amazon queen, Penthesilea, whom he has mortally wounded.

She pledged her support to King Priam of Troy and prepared for battle in the Trojan War alongside her personal guard of twelve fellow Amazons (Antibrote, Ainia, Clete, Alcibie, Antandre, Bremusa, Derimacheia, Derinoe, Harmothoe, Hippothoe, Polemusa and Thermodosa).

Rising early on her first (and last) day of battle, she prepared herself. Determined to redeem her soul, she channelled her rage against Achilles, who had killed the Trojan prince Hector, and vowed to dispatch him. It must have been one hell of a hand-to-hand fight between two epic warriors, especially considering one

Bronze Bust of an Amazon, Metropolitan Museum of Art.

was the daughter of the god of war and the other was, apart from his 'heel', immortal.

Ultimately, however, Penthesilea died at Achilles' hand as he thrust his sword through her breast and impaled her. Removing her helmet, Achilles fell completely in love with her. (Or, as other stories have it, he committed necrophilia and had sex with her corpse.)

Fellow Greek solider Thersites mocked Achilles for his romantic weakness. Achilles then, in a 'Hulk punches Thor' moment, killed him. In revenge for that (you can see where the phrase 'Greek tragedy' comes in handy) Thersites' cousin Diomedes fixed Penthesilea's body to the back of his chariot, dragged it to the Scamander River and unceremoniously dumped it. Achilles retrieved it and returned it to the Trojans for its rightful burial.

Poignantly, her name means 'mourned by the people', from the Greek words 'penthos' and 'laos' and her story became a firm favourite amongst Greek vase painters.

Artemisia of Caria
(aka Artemisia I)

'I pass over all the other officers [of the Persians] because there is no need for me to mention them, except for Artemisia, because I find it particularly remarkable that a woman should have taken part in the expedition against Greece. She took over the tyranny after her husband's death, and although she had a grown-up son and did not have to join the expedition, her manly courage impelled her to do so…Hers was the second most famous squadron in the entire navy, after the one from Sidon. None of Xerxes' allies gave him better advice than her.' (VII.99)

Herodotus, Battle of Salamis

Also known as Queen Caria I, born sometime during the fifth century BCE, Artemisia is known for her exploits as the only female commander during the Greek-Persian wars - and also the world's first known female captain of a naval fleet. She was named after the Goddess of the Hunt, Artemis, who was sister to Apollo.

Her father was the King of Halicarnassus and her mother was from Crete; typically, at a time when most women were anonymous, we don't know the name of her mother. That we even know of Artemisia (most of the information comes from her fellow Halicarnassusian, the historian Herodotus, aka the Father of History) speaks volumes about her exploits and her reputation.

She was married off to the King of Caria (part of Persia located in modern Turkey) who died in mysterious circumstances and whose name we also don't know, leaving her with a young son, Pisindelis. She took over as Regent for her son, running the

kingdom which also included the nearby islands of Kos, Nisyros and Kalymnos.

Immortalised in the film *300 Rise of an Empire*, her character is vividly brought to life by the incredible Eva Green, who says that whilst researching the character, 'I found out that she was very different from the movie. She was a very brave woman commander, but she was in love with Xerxes, so it's a completely different story. And I kind of got inspired more by Cleopatra, or Lady Macbeth, you know, kind of bloodthirsty characters…'

Artemisia fought for Xerxes and together with the five ships she brought to the fight, was the naval commander and brilliant tactician in the Persian navy against the Greeks during the Battle of Salamis in 480 BC. Ruthless in battle, she would carry two flags on board, one Greek and the other Persian. On approaching a Greek ship, she'd fly their flag on her own vessel to fool them, then attack.

Her ally Xerxes, watching the battle from his throne on top of Mount Egaleo, refused to take her advice to continue the fight against the Greeks on land. He attacked the Greek fleet again by sea on 29 September 480BC and Artemisia had no choice but to fight for him again.

The Greeks were seriously annoyed that Artemisia was waging war against them and offered a reward 10,000 drachmas for her capture. The reward was never claimed.

The brother of Xerxes, an admiral in the fleet, was killed in battle and Artemisia was tasked with retrieving the body. She deliberately smashed one of her own ships into a Persian one, in order to fool the oncoming Greeks that she was one of them. At this audacious manoeuvre, Xerxes is rumoured to have exclaimed, 'My men fight like women, and my women like men!'

Ultimately however, having ignored her military advice, Xerxes suffered a dreadful defeat at the Battle of Salamis. He trusted Artemisia so implicitly that he allowed her to accompany his illegitimate children to Ephesus on the Ionian coast (also modern Turkey). Maddeningly, after that she disappears from historical record.

Herodotus, wrote in his *Histories*:

> 'Her brave spirit and manly daring sent her forth to
> the war, when no need required her to adventure. Her
> name, as I said, was Artemisia.'

Her death remains a mystery, although some unsubstantiated reports, which are not even remotely in keeping with what we know of her character, suggest she threw herself off a cliff in an act of unrequited love for a younger man called Dardanus.

Boudicca/Boadicea
(died c. AD 60/61)

Boudicca statue on Westminster Bridge, London, sculpted by Thomas Thornycroft and erected in 1902.

History has no record of the name she was born with - Boudicca, meaning 'Victory' is the name given to her when she fought the Romans. What we know of her is only from three Roman historical sources, two by historian Tacitus and the third by another historian, Dio Cassius. There are no written records from the Celts to either confirm or deny any of it.

This much we know: Queen of the Iceni, Boudicca is described as tall and fearsome with masses of red hair and she led a huge rebellion against the Romans, who referred to her as 'The Killer Queen'. She was married to Prasutagus and together they ruled the Iceni tribe of East Anglia.

As they invaded and conquered the south of Britain, the Romans allowed the Iceni to continue. Prasutagus, hoping to keep the Romans onside and sweet, made Emperor Nero co-heir of his lands, together with his daughters. It proved to be a very short-term fix.

After Prasutagus died, the Romans decided they'd be in charge and that their laws prohibited his inheritance to pass down to his daughters. They plundered and confiscated the land, cattle and riches of the Iceni. After flogging Boudicca, they proceeded to flog and rape her daughters in front of her. This act of public brutality would have been viewed as sacrilege; the Romans wanted to desecrate any air of divine mystique around them as women and Celtic royals.

The Roman historian, Tacitus, wrote:

> '[Her] kingdom was plundered by centurions, his house by slaves, as if they were the spoils of war. First, his wife Boudicea was scourged [flogged], and his daughters outraged. All the chief men of the Iceni, as if Rome had received the whole country as a gift, were stripped of their ancestral possessions, and the king's relatives were made slaves...'

Around AD 60 or 61, the Iceni decided they'd had enough of being treated as slaves. Joined by other tribes, including the Trinovantes, who were equally furious and disgruntled, and under Boudicca's leadership, they rebelled in their tens of thousands. Boudicca's daughters would be by her side every step of the way; her soldiers smashed the Roman Ninth Legion and captured the legionary base of Camulodunum, (now Colchester), destroying a Roman temple.

Tacitus says:

> 'The whole island [of Britain] now rose up under the leadership of Boudicca, a queen, for Britons make no distinction of sex in their appointment of commanders.'

Not half way done yet, they moved on to Londinium (London), where Tacitus says 70,000 were slaughtered and Verulamium, (St. Albans in Hertfordshire), destroying, burning and desecrating Roman cemeteries.

Roman historian Dio Cassius wrote that Boudicca was 'possessed of greater intelligence than is usually found in the female sex.'

She was finally defeated by Roman governor Gaius Suetonius Paullinus with his army of 10,000 from the 14th Legion at a battle thought to have taken place at Mancetter, near Nuneaton, in 61. Boudicca and her daughters rallied their Briton troops from their chariot and exhorted them to fight against their slavery.

She impressed Dio, who wrote:

> 'In stature she was very tall, in appearance most terrifying, in the glance of her eye most fierce, and her voice was harsh; a great mass of the tawniest hair fell to her hips; around her neck was a large golden necklace; and she wore a tunic of divers colours over which a thick mantle was fastened with a brooch. This was her invariable attire ...'

Dio added that she clutched a spear when she spoke to her people.

What happened next was bloody in the extreme. Outnumbered and out manoeuvred, the rebels were slaughtered in minutes. Tacitus reports that 80,000 Britons (men, women and children) were massacred although this figure is almost certainly a wild exaggeration. The Romans lost 400 men. It is thought that rather than be captured, Boudicca and her daughters poisoned themselves.

Dio tells us:

> 'Two cities were sacked, eighty thousand of the Romans and of their allies perished, and the island was lost to Rome. Moreover, all this ruin was brought upon the Romans by a woman, a fact which in itself caused them the greatest shame.'

In 1902, Boudicca had her own bronze statue erected next to London's Westminster Bridge; depicted by artist Thomas Thorneycroft forever riding in her chariot, she remains a symbol of female strength and power and the fight for freedom.

Khutulun (1260-1306)

Khutulun (meaning: moonlight) was a warrior princess, Mongolian nomad, wrestler, archer, collector of horses and the great great grand-daughter of the legendary Genghis Khan. She was the daughter of Kaidu, (a cousin of Kublai Khan), who had 14 sons and other daughters – but Khutulun is the only one who made history. Mongolian women were known for being strong, athletic and utterly brilliant horsewomen. There must have been many more who could have made the history books but weren't blessed with the advantages of her birth.

Unfortunately, as happens in all families, there was a disagreement between Kublai and Kaidu; clearly, they could hold a serious grudge as this one lasted for three decades. By the time she was 20, her father was the most powerful ruler of Central Asia and she helped him keep out unwanted Mongolian invaders sent by Kublai.

Marco Polo, who met Khutulun in 1280, described her thus:

> 'Sometimes she would quit her father's side, and make a dash at the host of the enemy, and seize some man thereout, as deftly as a hawk pounces on a bird, and carry him to her father; and this she did many a time.'

These acts were random but scared the hell out of their opponents. Travel writers such as Rashid al-Din also wrote of her exploits.

Khutulun was utterly fearless, a skilled tactician and her father adored her, often seeking her advice and support. When he died, she guarded his tomb.

A skilled rider and undefeated wrestler (of both men and women), she even challenged potential suitors for her hand to beat

her at wrestling; if they won, she'd marry them; if they lost, they'd give her either 10 or 100 horses. Let's just say she ended up with a lot of horses (around 10,000).

Her enemies spread a lot of gossip about her alleged incestuous relationship with her father; they made out that was the real reason she refused to marry. In order to firmly quash those rumours and to support her father, she eventually did marry. Little is known of her husband apart from his name (Abtakul) and the fact that she didn't wrestle him – she chose him.

Her father wanted her to become leader of the Khan but her 14 brothers, who weren't so progressive in their thinking, weren't having any of it. She happily settled for being leader of the army instead.

She died at the age of 46.

Joan of Arc (c. 1412-30 May 1431)

'I am not afraid. I was born to do this.'

No self-respecting list of heroic women would be complete without Joan, aka the martyred Maid of Orleans. Born around 1412 and burnt at the stake in 1431, Joan's real name could have been Jehanne d'Arc, Jehanne Tarc, Jehanne Romée or possibly Jehanne de Vouthon.

She grew up an illiterate peasant in north eastern France, in a village called Domremy; her father was a farmer and her mother, Isabelle Romée, was an extremely observant Catholic who passed on her love for her faith to her daughter.

Joan took a vow of chastity and refused to accept a marriage her father had arranged for her. Legend has it that she heard voices and had visions – symptoms perhaps of what modern medicine would classify as anything from schizophrenia and bipolar disorder to bovine tuberculosis – urging her to cut her hair into the now famous bob and drive the English from France.

She had zero military experience but was persuasive enough to convince Prince Charles of Valois to let her lead an army to Orleans, the French town besieged by the English. Legend has it that Charles agreed to take Joan's advice after a private meeting between the two, where Joan revealed information to the future king that could only have come from God. Whatever was said, he emerged as seemingly convinced as she was that she would crown him king at Rheims. They won a decisive victory resulting in the prince being crowned King Charles VII in 1429.

Joan wanted to continue and retake Paris but with her position of favour on the wane, the king was persuaded otherwise.

Interestingly for a woman remembered as a fighter, Joan, dressed in white armour and riding on a white horse, never actually

Joan of Arc, painted by Jules Bastien-Lepage, 1879.

fought, although she was wounded twice. She was more of a strategist and token mascot to inspire bravery and heroism in the French armies of Charles VII in the battles between the French and English during the One Hundred Years War.

At the king's command, in 1430 she set off to fight the forces of Burgundy at Compiegne. She was captured outside the city gates by the English and taken to the castle of Bouvreuil. Charles did nothing to save her. He dumped her like a tonne of bricks and left her to rot as a prisoner, chained to her bed, for a year, to face the inquisitors, who couldn't break her spirit or find her guilty of heresy or witchcraft.

She might have been a teenager but she didn't hesitate to school her elders for swearing or missing Mass. During her trial at Rouen, (she had 70 charges against her, including witchcraft) when asked by a churchman what languages the 'voices' in her head spoke, she furiously retorted that they no doubt spoke better French than he did.

She eventually caved in, denied she'd had divine intervention and signed her confession. But stubborn and contrary to the end, she reneged a few days later and dressed herself once more in men's garb, resulting in her conviction as a relapsed heretic. In the end, her fate would be decided on the basis of her cross-dressing - something her captors argued went against the Bible. The English burnt her at the stake in Rouen on 30 May 1431. She would actually be burnt at the stake a total of three times in order for her organs and body to be completely destroyed. Her ashes were allegedly found in 1867 in the attic of a Parisian apothecary but tests proved them to be fake (and actually the remains of an Egyptian mummy and a cat); they remain in a museum dedicated to Joan in Chinon.

It would take twenty years for Charles to order a re-trial to restore Joan's reputation. She was canonized as a saint in 1920 and her legend immortalised in art, literature and film.

'One life is all we have and we live it as we believe in living it. But to sacrifice what you are and to live without belief, that is a fate more terrible than dying.'

Caterina Sforza (1463-28 May 1509) aka the Lioness of the Romagna, Lady of Imola, Countess of Forli

A Renaissance warrior woman and contemporary of the Borgia family and Machiavelli, Caterina was the illegitimate offspring of the Duke of Milan, Galeazzo Maria Sforza (murdered when she was 14) and his mistress Lucrezia Landriani.

The Duke recognised Caterina as his own and she was raised in his household. Her stepmother Bona of Savoy ensured her charge received a proper education. She spent time at the Milanese Court and was betrothed by proxy at the age of ten; the marriage would take place when she was 14.

Giralomo Riario, her 29-year-old betrothed, whilst quite a catch politically as the nephew of Pope Sixtus IV, was rather lacking in the personality department. However, they had eight children, (six of whom survived) and lived very comfortably in Rome, safe under the patronage of the Pope. Things were all fine and dandy until the Pope's death in 1484, which meant that, politically, they fell from grace.

Seven months pregnant with her sixth child, Caterina rode on horseback, in full armour, to the fortress of Castel Sant'Angelo, where the Cardinals were due to arrive to choose the next Pope. Determined to ensure that she kept her lands and properties, she refused to let them in, until they promised that the cities and titles of Imola and Forli would go directly to her husband. She held onto the Castel for eleven days in October 1484.

Whilst her bravery was admirable, her husband's conduct on governing the city wasn't. It didn't make him popular. No one likes a huge tax hike (some things never change) and he was murdered

Presumed portrait of Caterina Sforza, by Lorenzo di Credi, (c. 1481-1483).

by no less than nine men whilst Caterina and her children were seized and held prisoners in Forli. Her revenge was violent and without mercy – members of the rival Orsi family, thought to be responsible for the murder, were themselves either executed in public or strangled in secret.

Her second marriage, in August 1495, was to Giacomo Feo, the brother of the garrison commander of her castle. Eventually he too was brutally assassinated and the revenge she meted out was horrific. Not just the assassins, but their families, children and mistresses - stories abound that they were flung in a well and left to die.

Marriage number three in 1496 was to Giovanni de Medici, but he died of gout two years later and shortly after the birth of their only child together.

In 1499, she came up against the legendary Cesare Borgia in a dispute over land. According to Machiavelli, when faced with his armies and their threat to murder her son, she raised her skirts and screamed that as a woman, she could always make more babies: 'Ho con me lo stampo per farne degli altri!' (I have the equipment to bear more!).

She put up one hell of a fight but lost, was raped by Cesare and ended up back in prison at Castel Sant'Angelo where she remained for 18 months, before her release in 1501; but not before being accused of sending poisoned letters (infected with the plague) to the Pope. She would go on to fight to regain her lands in Imola and Forli but the cities refused to have her back.

She was the author of Gli Experimenti, the Experiments, a famous and well-respected tome on alchemy, the more remarkable for the time it was written in, as she was a female author. It included recipes for cosmetics, alchemy and medicines. Her descendants include grandson Cosimo I de Medici, great granddaughter Isabella de Medici, King Charles II of England and Diana, Princess of Wales.

Towards the end of her life, she remarked to a monk in Florence, 'If I were to write the story of my life, I would shock the world.'

She died of influenza on 28 May 1509.

Grace O'Malley (1530-1603) Gráinne Ní Mháille, aka Grace O'Malley, Queen of Umail and the Pirate Queen of Ireland

The sixteenth century saw the rise of two queens, both fearless, ruthless and awe-inspiring – you would not want to mess with either of these formidable women. They were Queen Elizabeth I and the relatively unknown Grace O'Malley, chieftain of the west coast of Ireland. Tensions between the Gaelic Irish and the English would bring those two women face to face.

Grace's tenacious spirit was evident from an early age. When her father, chieftain of the kingdom of Umhall, banned her from sailing with him on a trading expedition, she refused to take no for an answer. Her mother wrung her hands and warned her wayward daughter that her long hair would get trapped in the ropes. Grace responded by chopping off her hair and boarding the merchant ship – problem solved. This wasn't just an isolated teenage transgression; this was a sign of the fierce, independent women she would become – from teen to OAP rebel.

Grace O'Malley was the sort of woman you admire but may not cosy up with. She was of the Enid Blyton and games teacher ilk – the pull yourself up by the boot straps and get on with it type. Swashbuckling tales and legends abound about Grace, such as one about a sea battle where she admonishes her son to stop cowardly hiding behind her petticoats whilst she brandishes swords and fury. She wasn't a fan of maternity leave either, as just one day after giving birth on her ship she took up arms to defend it before berating useless men who couldn't let her have one day off without needing her.

She was a fiercely protective mother hen guarding not just her own children but also her vast brood of clansmen. Gaelic Ireland was disintegrating and being swallowed up by Tudor England. The clans that had enjoyed autonomy were fighting the English, fighting each other or giving in and swearing fealty to Henry VIII as their king in return for a title and land.

Grace's family being of the same tough bootstrap gene pool were disgusted by those who appeased the English and when the patriarchal Gaelic system tried to stop Grace inheriting her father's ships, she soon put paid to their misogynistic nonsense by showing her fearsome mettle.

She was in charge of hundreds of men and a fleet of ships as well as commanding an army to protect her land from the English. In a highly successful highway robbery of the seas, her men would demand 'tax' from ships that sailed in their waters. Refusal turned the seawater red, earning her such a fearsome reputation that the English decided it was time to deal with the Gaelic Pirate Queen.

After laying siege to her castle in Rockfleet in 1574, the English soon turned tail and ran after she chased them off. They now saw her as a serious threat to the anglicising of Ireland and their hope for a shiny new green land. Sir Richard Bingham, the English governor of Connaught, was more tenacious and succeeded in taking her castle, cattle and basically making a rather dangerous nuisance of himself. So what do you do when middle management doesn't listen? You bypass them for the big boss. Grace took herself

The meeting of Grace O'Malley and Queen Elizabeth I (an illustration from Anthologia Hibernica, vol. 11, 1793).

off to London to plead her case to Queen Elizabeth I, a bold move as she was a wanted pirate facing a gruesome execution from a queen who was not known for her forgiving nature.

Grace was a canny lass and could play court politics with the best of them, and somehow persuaded the good queen to order her castle and lands be handed back to her and to legitimise her seafaring 'business'. There may have been some agreement that Grace would help keep the even more 'annoying' Spanish at bay, but, as ever, there are few records left to say exactly what went on.

Sources claim that Grace realised quite correctly that her new pal Elizabeth was likely to renege on the deal. However, Grace managed to live to a ripe old age and died in around 1603 in Rockfleet Castle. Her legend continues to this day.

Catalina de Erauso (1585/92-1650) aka the Lieutenant Nun

Catalina was a seventeenth century escapee nun who spent twenty years living as a man. Her autobiography claims she was born in 1585; however, baptism records give the date as 1592. Her father Miguel de Araujo was a Basque officer and Catalina shared his military ambition. However, in news that will shock none of you, this was a time when options for women were extremely limited.

Gender roles were rigidly defined, especially in a typically traditional and distinguished Catholic family from which she came. Like her three sisters, Catalina was left at a convent run by her prioress aunt either, depending on the source, as a baby, or when she was around four years old, for her education and well-being. The convent was in San Sebastian in the Basque area of Spain. Her sisters would spend the rest of their lives within its confines whilst the girls' brothers set off for the Americas to make their fortune.

DOÑA CATALINA DE ERAUSO.

Catalina was never going to do as she was told or be married off like a good Spanish girl. She was sent to the monastery of San Bartolome to become a nun. The beatings she received there in an attempt to 'break' her failed miserably. True to her rebellious spirit, she escaped on 19 March 1600, when she was 15, determined to make her own life as a man. It was the only route open to her to live on her own terms.

Cutting her hair and dramatically altering her convent clothing into a pair of breeches, she adopted a male identity and persona. Incredibly, she would encounter - and fail to be recognised by - several members of her own family, including her father. Calling herself Alonso Díaz Ramírez de Guzmán, she would take on several jobs before joining the Spanish army as a soldier in the forces led by Captain Gonzalo Rodríguez, left for the Americas as a conquistador when she was 18, went to war in Chile to try to civilise the Mapuche and rose to the rank of lieutenant only to be suspended from soldiering for killing a Mapuche leader.

To say that Catalina lived a full life would be a dramatic understatement. Details of her exploits are sourced mainly from her own 'autobiography', *Vida I Sucesos de la Monja Alférez*, written in 1624. Roughly translated as *the Life and Times of a Lieutenant Nun*, in it she mostly refers to herself as 'he'. In today's society, she'd probably be considered a lesbian or a transgender man, the concepts of which obviously didn't exist at the time. During her life, she would use different names, from Pedro de Orive, and Alonso Díaz to Antonio de Erauso. If caught cross dressing, the penalties would have been severe.

She travelled to Panama and Peru, was imprisoned, got into fights and drunken brawls, gambled and was a fugitive from the law. She'd also have a variety of jobs, one of which 'she' was fired from for engaging in amorous pursuits with her employer's sister in law, apparently 'running his hand between her legs'. Living as a man, 'he' was something of a rogue, becoming engaged to two unsuspecting women at the same time, and then absconding with both their dowries.

Incredibly, one of the soldiers she had to report to was her own brother, Don Miguel de Erauso, who didn't even recognise her, and who she later tragically killed in a duel.

Her eventual fifteen hour confession to a priest, the Bishop of Guamanga, to save herself from capture, also reads like a very good work of fiction:

'Sir, all this I have told your Lordship is not so. The truth is this: that I am a woman; that I was born in such-and-such a place, daughter of such-and-such man and woman; that I was placed at a certain age in such-and-such a convent with my aunt so-and-so; that I grew up there, took the habit and became a novice; that, about to take the vows, I ran off; that I went to such-and-such a place, stripped, dressed myself as a man, cut off my hair, travelled here and there, went to sea, roamed, hustled, corrupted, maimed, and murdered, until coming to end up here at his Lordship's feet'.

It's seriously good stuff, made all the more dramatic by her subsequent physical examination by two midwives who, whilst probably shocked out of their minds, confirmed, that 'he' was in fact a 'she'. Most importantly to them, and the authorities, she was 'intact': a virgin. So despite the murdering, the plundering, the soldiering, the womanising and the cross-dressing, because she was still 'untouched', all was forgiven.

Catalina created a public sensation on her eventual return to Spain and in 1625 she had the chutzpah to ask King Felipe IV for a pension in recognition of her military service. The King agreed: she was granted 800 pesos per annum. She was forgiven for the sin of cross dressing and Pope Urban VIII gave his permission for her to continue her life as a man; no doubt the fact that she had been fighting for the Catholic faith – and was still 'intact' – played a part in his largesse.

Taking the name Antonio de Erauso, living and dressing as a man, she eventually settled in Mexico, setting up business as a mule driver between Veracruz and Mexico City. She died of a heart attack in 1650. Her memoir was published nearly two hundred years after her death, in 1829.

Ulricka Eleonora Stålhammar
(c.1688-16 February 1733)

Ulricka was a cross dresser and Swedish female soldier who fought in the Great Northern War. She was born into a military family and following the death of their father, Lieutenant-Colonel Johan Stålhammar, in 1711, she and her five sisters were left in impoverished circumstances and heavily reliant on the charity of friends and family.

An accomplished rider and hunter, determined not to be forced into a loveless marriage of convenience in order to help their financial dire straits, in 1713 Ulricka had a rummage in her father's wardrobe, dressed herself as a man, stole a horse and ran away.

She joined the Swedish army in 1713 and remained there for thirteen years during the Great Northern War between King Karl XII of Sweden and Tsar Peter the Great, referring to herself as Vilhelm or William Edstedt. She operated the cannons as an artillerist and was promoted to Corporal. Sweden would eventually capitulate in 1721.

In 1716 she met and fell in love with the maid – Maria Lönnman. They subsequently got married (with Ulricka wearing the trousers in the relationship) but the marriage was never sexually consummated. Maria apparently was completely ignorant of her husband's true gender.

When in 1724, Ulricka's sister Katarina, a devout Christian, discovered the marital deception, she was furious and threatened to expose her sister. In an attempt to 'atone' for her behaviour, and to convince her sister that she was sorry, Ulricka left the army in 1726. In order to reintroduce herself to women's clothes after a twelve year absence, she left for Denmark for two years, leaving Maria to work for a family relative.

In 1728, after writing a penitent letter of apology to the Swedish government for her alleged crimes, Ulricka returned to Sweden, only to be arrested. She decided to confess the truth about her

Museum exhibit featuring Ulricka Eleonora Stålhammar.

gender to her wife but it was irrelevant to Maria; the couple truly loved each other and remained married until Ulricka's death years later. Whilst the court found it difficult to decide what to charge the couple with, they eventually decided on 'breaking the law of God and Nature' by marrying a member of the same sex and violating the order of God by cross-dressing.

The court believed they hadn't actually committed any homosexual acts (consummated the marriage), and Maria insisted she thought her husband had been impotent. Maria said she was a survivor of rape and content to abstain from sex within her marriage. Ulricka underwent a medical examination and apart from having un-developed breasts, was confirmed to be a female.

In their infinite wisdom, the judges believed that their love was a spiritual union rather than sexual. They were sentenced to one month (William/Ulricka) and 12 days (Maria) in prison. There was no punishment for her having served as a man in the army; apparently, her stellar military record spoke for itself and wasn't in dispute. The then monarch, Frederick I, followed the case closely and insisted that Ulricka had a relatively comfortable time during her brief incarceration.

They were, however, forbidden to live together again. Maria would go back to working as a maid for her 'husband's' wealthy aunt whilst William, now Ulricka once more, lived with another set of relatives. Living on different family estates, the correspondence between the two survives and remains testament to the enduring and genuine love between the two women. Ulricka would die at the age of 45, survived by Maria for another twenty-eight years.

No images of her survive but Ulrica's story is not an isolated one; there are several tales of Swedish women dressing as men in order to fight for their country, namely Margareta von Ascheberg, Margareta Elisabeth Roos and Anna Jöransdotter.

Nakano Takeko - (1846/47-1868)

Only relatively recently have historians realised the wider military contributions of female samurai; most likely because an army recording that a battle had been won with the support of women warriors would have taken the glory away from the men. Just as recent archaeological evidence points towards Viking women fighting alongside the men as equals, and a shift in historical evidence of gender roles in the military, an excavation and DNA tests at the Battle of Senbon Matsubara (between Takeda Katsuyori and Hojo Ujinao in 1580) reveal that 35 of the 105 bodies were women.

Nakano was a Japanese warrior and female samurai who fought in the Boshin War – a battle between the Tokugawa shogunate and supporters of the Imperial Court.

The daughter of Aizu official Nakano Heinai, she spent five years as an adopted daughter under the tutelage of her martial arts teacher, Akaoka Daisuke, who also taught her literature and mathematics. But in 1868, Akaoka remembered Nakano was a woman and tried to organise a marriage for her with his nephew. If that wedding had gone ahead, we'd likely never have heard of Nakano again. However, she refused, returned to Aizu and set herself up as a martial arts teacher.

In the midst of the Boshin War, the Shogun surrendered in May 1868, but forces loyal to him continued to fight, retreating back to Aizu. Nakano joined the battle against the forces of the Imperial court in a siege that lasted a month.

Strictly speaking, the women of Aizu weren't allowed to fight, but Nakano disregarded this and formed a samurai squad, a band of twenty determined women warriors, including her own mother and sister, Nakano Yuko, all determined to end the siege. They were trained with the naginata, a perfect weapon for the women owing to its long reach, an important counter-balance against enemies who might be heavier or stronger.

Nakano was ferocious in the heart of the battle, killing five Imperial soldiers before succumbing to a bullet to the chest. Determined that her body wouldn't be used as a trophy, she asked her sister to remove her head and bury it. She did so, beneath a pine tree at the Hōkai-ji Temple. There is now a memorial there in her honour and her memory is revered by the modern young women of Aizu.

Mariya Oktyabrskaya
(16 August 1905-15 March 1944)

One of ten children born to a poor Ukranian peasant family, Mariya was a communist who took part in the Russian revolution. Her husband (they married in 1925) was a revolutionary himself. Trained as a nurse and a member of the Military Wives Council, she learned how to use weapons and machinery. After her country was invaded by the Nazis, she was evacuated to Siberia. Her husband stayed to fight and was killed. She didn't find out for two whole years and when she did, she was determined to repay the favour in kind.

She wrote to her sister: 'I've had my baptism by fire. . . Sometimes I'm so angry I can't even breathe.' On eventually learning that her husband had fallen during the Battle of Kiev, she sold all her possessions to buy a brand new tank for the army. Her one stipulation was that she would drive it herself. This is what she wrote to Stalin:

> 'My husband was killed in action defending the motherland. I want revenge on the fascist dogs for his death and for the death of Soviet people tortured by the fascist barbarians. For this purpose I've deposited all my personal savings – 50,000 roubles – to the National Bank in order to build a tank. I kindly ask to name the tank "Fighting Girlfriend" and to send me to the front line as a driver of said tank.'

Subsequently painting the name 'Fighting Girlfriend' in Russian on the side, she joined the 26th Guard Tank Brigade.

The olive-green 26-ton T-34 Main Battle Tank was one hell of a war machine. She learned to drive and maintain it during three

months of training. Extremely hands on, she would climb out of her tank three times during her time as a driver and mechanic to fix it, often under enemy fire. On her first outing, she killed about 30 Nazi soldiers and completely destroyed an anti-tank gun. She was 38 and was swiftly promoted to Sergeant and fought in the Battle of Kursk in 1943.

Struck by an enemy artillery shell to the head in January 1944, which left her in a coma, she died two months later on 15 March.

She was Awarded the Gold Star of the Hero of the Soviet Union, the highest award for military bravery offered by the USSR.

Susan Travers
(23 September 1909-
18 December 2003)

Born in London on September 23 1909, Susan is the only woman to have ever joined the French Foreign Legion. A party-loving socialite living with her expat parents in the south of France, at the outbreak of the Second World War and looking for a clearer sense of purpose, she joined the French version of the Red Cross, the Croix Rouge. She would voluntarily spend the war as a driver with Free French legionnaires across North Africa and Europe.

In 1940, she went to Finland with the French expeditionary force as they fought in Russia. Whilst she was there, France fell to the Germans. She went to London and worked as a volunteer nurse with the Free French Forces of General Charles de Gaulle. Posted to Eritrea she drove ambulances, cars and trucks for senior officers, navigating her way through roads often lined with deadly mines.

Nicknamed 'La Miss' by the admiring fellow Legionnaires, she would drive for and fall madly in love with her senior (and very much married) French officer, Colonel Marie-Pierre Koenig, a war-hero who now has a Parisian square named in his honour.

They had a passionate, clandestine and ultimately short-lived love affair. At the Battle of Bir Hakeim in Libya in 1942, she would heroically drive Koenig straight through the encircled battle lines of the enemy. She did so under intense enemy artillery fire. The car took a battery of bullet holes, but she got him out safely, other soldiers following the path she forcibly created. Of the 3,700 troops who had been assigned to Bir Hakeim, nearly 2,500 survived because of her bravery.

Following her heroic endeavours, she was awarded the Croix de Guerre and the Ordre du Corps d'Arme, just two of the total of twelve medals she received during her lifetime.

Loath to return to her old life at the end of the war, in 1945 she completed an application form for the French Legion. She never wrote down her gender. She was accepted and served as a logistics officer until she resigned in 1947, when she married Foreign Legion non-commissioned officer, Nicholas Schlegelmilch; she destroyed her war diaries at the same time.

Awarded the Legion of Honour (France's highest accolade) in 1996, she died in Paris at the age of 94.

Lyudmila Pavlichenko
(1916-10 October 1974)

'Every German who remains alive will kill women,
children and old folks. Dead Germans are harmless.
Therefore, if I kill a German, I am saving lives.'

During the Second World War, Russia recruited around 2000 women
as snipers, 500 of whom survived. At 25, Ukrainian Lyudmila
Pavlichenko, aka Lady Death, remains the most successful female
sniper in history. Serving with the Red Army's 25th Rifle Division,
her weapon of choice was the M1891/30 Mosin-Nagant 7.62 mm
rifle with a PE 4x telescope.

Ukrainian born, her father was a factory worker and her mother a
teacher. An avowed supporter of gender equality and women's rights,
Lyudmila was a history student at Kiev University. Determined to
excel in both her academic and physical pursuits, she enrolled at
sniper school at the age of 14, and also worked as a metal grinder in
a munitions factory.

The Nazis got her back up by invading Russia in June 1941. They
flattened her university and she wasted no time in signing up at the
recruiting office as a sniper. They tried to convince her to become a
nurse instead. She simply showed them her Voroshilov Sharpshooter
badge markmanship certificates and awards, which seemed to shut
them up!

She would kill 36 snipers in battles of counter-sniping (sniper vs
sniper) and a total of 309 people (mostly German soldiers) in her
short but incredible military career (187 in her first 75 days). The
real total is probably higher – for a 'kill' to be counted, it had to be
witnessed and during wartime there was no way to account for every
Nazi she took out.

She refused to count her first two kills (Romanians working with the Germans) as they were 'test shots' set as an audition by the Red Army to gauge her skill with a rifle. Such was her reputation that after stints in Odessa and Moldova, by the Siege of Sevastopol, (on the Crimean peninsula) the Germans actually knew her by name. They'd send out messages on their radio loudspeakers, inviting her to join them and trying to sweeten the deal by offering her plenty of chocolate.

Targeted whilst hiding in a tree, she deliberately fell out of it and played dead for hours before resuming duties.

Sevastopol eventually fell after eight horrific months. She was hit by a mortar shell, evacuated by submarine, promoted to Major and given a new job as a sniper instructor. Left behind, the majority of her unit, including her husband Sergeant-Major Leonid Kitsenko, were killed. Later, recuperating from her wounds, shrapnel to her face and shell shock, she was sent to the US to be the poster-woman for the Soviets and help push for their support for a Second Front.

US First Lady Eleanor Roosevelt took the younger woman, dressed in her army uniform and speaking not a word of English, under her wing. She was the first Soviet citizen to visit the White House. In 1942 she embarked on a speaking tour of 43 cities across

the US to support Stalin's war effort and talk about her experiences as a female soldier.

The US press simply referred to her as the 'Girl Sniper' and were more interested in reporting whether or not she wore makeup and how stylish (or not) her uniform was. After one too many such 'silly' questions about her nail polish and how she styled her hair, as well as press stories about how her army skirt made her fat and how she attacked copious amounts of American food with gusto, her icy reserve shattered. She said to *Time* magazine in no uncertain terms:

> 'I wear my uniform with honor. It has the Order of Lenin on it. It has been covered with blood in battle. It is plain to see that with American women what is important is whether they wear silk underwear under their uniforms. What the uniform stands for, they have yet to learn.'

In Chicago, now fully in command of herself, she said:

> 'Gentlemen, I am 25 years old and I have killed 309 fascist occupants by now. Don't you think, gentlemen, that you have been hiding behind my back for too long?'

She spent the rest of the war training other snipers; at the end of it, she completed her Master's degree in history and worked as a military historian. She was awarded her country's highest honour (the Gold Star Medal) and given the title of 'Hero of the Soviet Union'. She would also feature on two commemorative stamps.

Fifteen years later, in 1957, Eleanor Roosevelt was touring Moscow and asked to see her old friend. She discovered Lyudmila had remarried, borne two children and was living quietly in a modest flat. Despite being accompanied by minders who prevented them from acting normally, Lyudmila grabbed Eleanor's hand and ran into the bedroom. With the door firmly shut against their minders, the two women had a long overdue and emotional catch-up like the old friends they were.

Faye Schulman
(November 28, 1919 -)

Born in Lenin, Poland, Faye grew up in today's Belarus. When Germany and the Russians partitioned Poland in 1939, her place of birth was handed over to the Russians.

She is one of the only known Jewish partisan photographers during the Second World War to capture images of life in the forest. Her brother Moishe, also a photographer, taught her the basics of taking, processing and developing pictures.

The Nazis murdered 1850 Jews from the Lenin ghetto on August 14, 1942, including Faye's parents, younger brother and her sisters. They only spared her (amongst a total of 26 that day) because of her ability with a camera. They made her develop the pictures they had taken of that day's massacre. Unbeknownst to the Germans, she developed a secret set for herself, for history to remember.

Escaping to the forests, she joined the Moldova brigade, made up of Soviet Red Army prisoners of war who had escaped, and worked as a nurse for them from September 1942 until July 1944; she had zero medical training.

It was during the brigade's raid on Lenin that she retrieved her photographic equipment and she knew exactly how she'd use it. In between brigade work, she spent two years taking over one hundred photographs, hiding her camera whilst on missions:

> 'I want people to know that there was resistance. Jews did not go like sheep to the slaughter. I was a photographer. I have pictures. I have proof.'

Her images are a devastating indictment of a horrific period in history but also testament to the camaraderie between the partisans. One

picture shows Jewish fighters being buried alongside their Russian comrades; another depicts a group, including Faye, happily reuniting, each having believed the other had perished.

At the end of the war, Faye married fellow Jewish partisan Morris Schulman. After three years in the Landsberg Displaced Persons Camps in Germany, and with no desire to live in Poland, which they described as a 'graveyard', they immigrated to Canada in 1948.

Faye fought her own battle, not only to survive but to provide proof of Nazi atrocities and the Jewish struggle to fight back.

Hannah Szenes (Senesh)
(17 July 1921-7 November 1944)

Born in Budapest, Hungary, to a wealthy Jewish family, her father was a journalist and playwright (his influence clearly demonstrated in her keeping a regular diary for years) and her mother a housewife. Although the family was thoroughly assimilated into Hungarian society, Hannah experienced anti-Semitism for herself whilst at school – her family had to pay triple the fees of other students simply for being Jewish.

Undeterred by the hatred, she instead turned her energies into learning more about her Jewish heritage, joined a Zionist youth movement, learned Hebrew and emigrated to Palestine in 1939.

Of her immediate family, only her mother and brother would survive the Second World War.

After studying agriculture, she joined a kibbutz in Caesarea before being approached by members of the Jewish Agency. They wanted her for a secret military project, backed by the British – to get the Jews out of Nazi-occupied Europe to save them from the concentration camps and help captured Allied airmen.

She became a member of Palmah, (the underground Jewish military) learnt how to use radios and undertook a paratrooper course. The day before she left for Cairo for additional training by the British, she was reunited with her brother in Palestine for a few short hours. They would never see each other again.

The only woman of five Haganah members, Hannah was parachuted into Yugoslavia to support the forces fighting against the Nazis before crossing back over into her country of birth in June of 1944. Germany had invaded in March. She was captured and tortured in a Budapest prison but refused to reveal any information about her radio codes.

Her captors then arrested Hannah's mother Katharine and the two women were prisoners for three months. Although kept separate, it was the first time in five years the two had seen each other. Katherine, suddenly freed in September 1944, desperately sought legal help for her daughter, who as a Hungarian national, was tried as a traitor and sentenced to death for spying.

Whilst the court was in no hurry to carry out the sentencing, the military officer in charge, Colonel Simon, gave her two options: beg for mercy and a pardon or be shot. Hannah chose the latter. She refused the offer of a blindfold.

She was executed by firing squad at the age of 23 in Budapest and buried in a Jewish cemetery. A poem found in her cell reads:

> 'I gambled on what mattered most.
> The dice were cast. I lost.'

Her mother survived a death march from Budapest to Austria. She was determined that daughter's bravery should not be forgotten and together with her surviving son Giora, fought to have published Hannah's plays, diaries and poetry. Hannah's remains were brought to Israel in 1950 and buried alongside other parachutists in the military cemetery on Mount Herzl in Jerusalem.

WENCHES

Phryne the Thespian
(c 371-310 BC)

Phryne Before the Areopagus, by Jean-Baptiste-Henri Decays.

A Greek courtesan or hetaira born in the city of Thespiae in Boetia, Phryne is said to have won a court case by flashing her breasts. Her real name was Mnesarete, which meant 'commemorating virtue', but she was given the name Phryne, meaning 'toad' because of the sallow, yellow tinge of her skin.

Extremely beautiful, independent, educated and entertaining (the true embodiment of a hetaira and in complete contrast to the average Athenian woman) she was a model for painters and sculptors including Praxiteles, who became one of her clients. She was the inspiration and model for his nude statute of the Cnidian

Aphrodite, which became such a popular tourist attraction that the city had enough money to clear its entire debt; copies of the statue survive in the Vatican.

Phryne was a successful courtesan and made herself hugely wealthy, so much so that she offered to rebuild the walls of Thebes, (obliterated by Alexander the Great in 335 BCE) on the premise that her name be inscribed in them as such: 'destroyed by Alexander, restored by Phryne the courtesan'. Shocked that a woman, let alone a courtesan, could be even considered as the saviour of their glorious city, the government of Thebes refused, preferring to let the walls lie in ruin.

Phryne got naked at the Eleusis town festival dedicated to the god Poseidon and walked into the sea in his honour. The dramatic and bold act inspired the painter Apelles to create his picture 'Aphrodite Anadyomene'. The politicians however, weren't so impressed. They accused her of blasphemy and of impiety (*asebeia*), for daring to re-enact the sacred bathing rituals of Aphrodite in full naked view of Athenian society. They also accused her of promoting the cult of Isodaites (a deity, linked to both Pluto and Dionysus, and popular amongst Greek prostitutes). The punishment for such a crime was death. (Socrates was charged for impiety over fifty years earlier, for allegedly corrupting the young and believing in gods not approved by the state. He chose to kill himself by imbibing a lethal concoction of the poisonous plant hemlock). Phyrne was also likely charged because officials disapproved of her disrobing for so many artists, never mind how revered they were.

She was successfully defended by the lawyer (and client) Hyperides, a famed orator and politician from Athens with quite the predilection for hataera. Her prosecutor, Euthias, is rumoured to have been one of her former lovers, out to have his day in court at the expense of his rival Hyperides - but this of course could be purely conjecture.

The very nakedness which had so offended the council is said to have been her saving grace. Legend has it that she tore open her robe in the middle of her courtroom trial at the Areopagus, the city council of ancient Athens. Less X-rated version of the story simply have her shaking the hand of each and every member of the jury.

Her reasoning for baring herself was that to sentence to death someone whose body had been sculpted as if by the gods, and in honour of Aphrodite herself, would be an affront to the gods' own divine sensibilities. Superstition also played a part in the eventual result of the trial; the jurors were terrified of the implications of insulting Aphrodite.

Whatever took place in the court room worked. Phryne was acquitted. And rumour has it that the outcome so infuriated Euthias that he never argued another legal case.

Her fellow hetaera Bacchis wrote a heartfelt letter of thanks to Hyperides:

> 'We courtesans are grateful to you, and each one of us is just as grateful as Phryne. The suit, to be sure… involved Phryne alone, but it meant danger for us all, for…if we…face prosecution for impiety, it's better for us to have done with this way of living…you have not merely saved a good mistress for yourself, but have put the rest of us in a mood to reward you on her account.'

Alice Perrers aka Alice de Windsor
(1348-1400)

Alice was the ruthless and highly ambitious mistress of Plantagenet King Edward III of England. She was also lady in waiting to his wife, Philippa of Hainault and thought to be the inspiration behind Geoffrey Chaucer's Wife of Bath in *The Canterbury Tales*.

Suffice to say that history and contemporary accounts do not treat her kindly. Before she came on the scene, the royal couple (married for 40 years) were said to have enjoyed a happy and contented marriage.

Alice became one of the richest and probably one of the most despised women in the country. She is described as being singularly ungifted in the looks department and was therefore accused of witchcraft by her detractors, for still being able to sexually and emotionally bewitch a feeble king who should have known better.

She was born in the 1340s, daughter of a Hertfordshire landowner although reports in the *St. Albans Chronicle*, (Sir Richard had an acrimonious dispute with St. Albans Abbey) claim her beginnings were much more humble, referring to her father as a tiler and her mother as a tavern whore.

Some time in the 1360s, Alice joined the Royal household; by 1366 she was one of the queen's ladies of the bedchamber.

Perrers seated beside King Edward III, being read to by Chaucer, imagined by artist Ford Madox Brown, painting exhibited in 1851.

Not wasting any time, she became the king's public mistress after the queen (who had thirteen children) died from the Black Death in 1369. Alice spent time with the king's two sons, Edward the Black Prince and John of Gaunt and allegedly used her influence to convince the king to hand over some of the late queen's jewellery; the whole collection amounted to £20,000, around £6 million today. By 1371, she was granted the manor of Wendover.

In 1375, she dressed as Lady of the Sun in a London tournament, riding in her own chariot, sumptuously and extravagantly dressed. She caused an absolute scandal.

She bore the King three children, John (later Sir John Southeray) and two daughters, Joan and Jane. Once Philippa was gone, Alice became head honcho at the royal court. Her power and influence were almost as immense as the dislike she inspired in others.

Being the king's mistress brought Alice huge financial rewards and bounty – land, jewels and lots of wine. As she rose in prominence and as the ailing king relied more heavily upon her counsel, she became the scapegoat for all the ills in the latter part of Edward's reign, particularly financial affairs, because he spent so much money on her and she had no problem enriching herself from the crown's coffers. She ended up with an estimated 56 properties across the country.

In 1376, when Alice would be one of those figures close to the king 'impeached' in what was known as the Good Parliament, medieval chronicler Walsingham said:

> '... the Parliamentary knights complained bitterly about one Alice Perrers, a wanton woman who was all too familiar with Edward III. They accused her of numerous misdeeds, performed by her and her friends in the realm. She far overstepped the bounds of feminine conduct: forgetful of her sex and her weakness, now besieging the king's justices, now stationing herself among the doctors in the ecclesiastical courts, she did not fear to plead in defence of her cause and even to make illegal demands. As a result of the scandal and

great shame which this brought on King Edward, not only in this kingdom but also in foreign lands, the knights sought her banishment from his side.'

The court would end up deciding that women be banned from playing any part in judicial decisions. Talk about a legal precedent!

As Edward grew older, Alice would look to the main chance – her future – and secretly arranged a marriage to William Windsor, Lord Lieutenant of Ireland, whilst still continuing as the king's mistress. When the arrangement was made public during the course of the Good Parliament, and the King seen as an adulterer, the people were appalled. William was held legally accountable and Alice banned from the king's sight. Banished from court, she was allowed back by her friend and ally John of Gaunt, the Duke of Lancaster and the late king's son.

History has not treated her kindly; there seems to be nothing lovable or even likeable about her. And it should be noted that all the accounts of her were written by men. On the king's death-bed, rumour has it that she removed the jewelled rings from his hands. (There are no images of her and indeed, all we have to go by is a rather biased picture of her doing just that).

Alice spent a lot of time and money defending herself in court, especially after her husband William's death in 1384. Her final years were spent fighting for her access to his fortune; he had left his entire estate to his three sisters. Clearly, he knew what he had married.

When she died, she was buried in the Church of St Lawrence in Upminster.

Imperia Cognati, the First Courtesan
(3 August 1486-15 August 1512)

Imperia La Divina was Queen of the Courtesans, celebrated sixteenth century Italian courtesan and lover of the rich, famous and powerful, a close and personal friend of Sienese banker Agostino Chigi, who in turn was an ally of Pope Alexander VI, aka Rodrigo de Borgia, father of Lucrezia, Cesare, Giovanni and Gioffre Borgia. Imperia's known lovers included papal librarians, poets, architects, painters and bankers. Her story features in a novella by contemporary writer Matteo Bandello.

She was probably born in Rome, the daughter of prostitute Diana di Pietro Cognati.

Courtiers of the Papal court started the courtesan trend by hiring highly educated, culturally and socially astute female prostitutes or escorts to join them in court as company. It worked for them – the courtiers weren't allowed to marry and the new elite band of 'courtesans' certainly weren't the marrying kind. Imperia is the first recorded Italian courtesan, who would pose seductively by their windows to show off their 'wares' to potential clients.

Aged just 17, she herself had a daughter, Lucrezia; the father was likely Agostino. Other customers included the papal secretary of Leo X.

Imperia is thought to have fatally poisoned herself aged just 26. Rumours abound as to the reason why – did her beloved client Angelo del Bufalo spurn her for another woman? Was she desperately threatened by the new and younger mistress of her chief patron Chigi? Or was she 'removed' due to an illicit affair with Pope Julius.

She left 25 ducats to each of her servants in her will and one hundred ducats to her mother; all of her property was given to daughter Lucrezia, whom she described as 'a chaste and modest virgin,

Statue of Imperia Cognati, at the entrance of the Konstanz harbour in Germany.

placed and at present residing, in the Venerable Convent of the nuns of S. Maria in Campo Marzio'.

Italian author and Imperia's contemporary Pietro Aretino insists she died rich, 'venerated and dignified in her own house', so much so that she was awarded a stately funeral in Rome – remarkable for a prostitute – and buried near the Colosseum.

A monument to her at Roman church San Gregorio al Celio sadly hasn't survived. An inscription on it, paid for by Chigi at a cost of a whopping 500 ducats, read: 'Imperia, Roman courtesan, who, worthy of such a great name, gave the example of a beauty rare among humans.'

Diane de Poitiers
(3 September 1499-25 April 1566)

A beautiful and powerful noblewoman in Renaissance France, the future mistress of Henri II of France made her court debut at the age of 16. It would be two decades later, now a widow and two decades older than the King, that she utterly entranced him.

Born in the castle of Saint-Vallier in the Swiss Alps, she was married to Louis de Breze, the grandson of Charles VII, at the age of 15. He would die in 1531, after which Diane became a companion to the sons of François I. She would become Henri's tutor and eventually, despite the age gap, they became lovers.

Catherine de Medici married Henri in 1533 – it was purely a political arrangement and Catherine would spend her wedded life utterly jealous of the hold Diane had over her husband. She tried to assert her authority and position, notably positioning a portrait of herself above Diane's own bed. (Catherine and Diane were actually distant relatives).

Henri gave Diane the estate of Chenonceau as a lasting and emphatic symbol of his love and devotion. It had originally been given to his wife, Catherine, so that must have stung.

When Henri became King in 1547, he was 30 and Diane was 47. He signed all his state documents 'HenriDiane'. Catherine was also nearly two decades younger than her rival. For years she failed to deliver an heir of any sort to the king and was on the verge of being sent packing back to Italy. It was Diane who intervened on her behalf and encouraged Henri to visit her bed chambers. It was probably a case of 'better the devil you know'. Diane knew what Catherine was all about. (Henri and Catherine would eventually have ten children). A new queen in her place could potentially create untold problems for her. Diane also nursed Catherine (who viewed Nostradamus as her personal astrologer) back to health when the latter fell prey to scarlet fever.

Diane's relationship with Henri made her arguably the most powerful woman in France. She was awarded the title Duchesse de Valentinois and given the crown jewels of France. Her style statement was to wear black and white and model herself on the Greek goddess of the hunt, Diana. Even in her sixties she continued to entrance the King.

Diane was fastidious about keeping a strict exercise regime to keep fit with horse riding and swimming. Her doctor, Ambroise Paré, suggested she bathe in cold water every morning to help fight off infection and boost her immune system.

In 1559, whilst wearing Diane's black and white 'favours' on his armour, Henri died of his wounds after a jousting accident. Despite the fact he died calling out for Diane, Catherine refused her access to him. She was also banned from his funeral. After his death, Catherine clawed back her power and banished Diane to the chateau in Anet which had been given to her by the King.

As a double whammy, she made her return all the crown jewels bestowed upon her by Henri. The Anet chateau still retains monograms of an intertwined D and H (Diane and Henri) amidst the architecture. The symbol can also still be seen in the Louvre, Fontainebleau, and the Paris Military Museum.

The special potion Diane drank to keep her young would be the death of her: made up of gold chloride and diethyl ether, it was death by gold poisoning at the age of 66. Buried in a black and white marble tomb, she stayed there for two hundred years, until the French Revolution, when her body was abruptly and violently exhumed. In her tomb were also the two bodies of two of her grandchildren. A monument would be built one hundred years later. The site would be excavated in 2008 and her bones carbon dated. The gold content of her bones was found to be at least 250 times higher than normal.

Mary Boleyn
(1499/1500-19 July 1543)

Mary's relationship with England's Henry VIII has always been overshadowed by that of her ambitious and ultimately doomed sister, Anne, who would fulfil her family's ruthless social ambition, marry the king and become queen of England, only to lose her head several years later. What history rarely focuses on is that when it comes to Henry VIII, Mary got in there first. The difference, however, is that she escaped with her life. Anne might have had the superior wit but she danced too close to the flames and was executed.

Mary was the oldest daughter of Thomas Boleyn and Elizabeth Howard, a lady in waiting to Queen Catherine of Aragon. She was born in Blickling Hall, Norfolk, followed by Anne in 1501 and then George, Thomas and Henry.

She was sent to France to be a lady in waiting to the Princess Mary Tudor, who was set to marry Louis XII. After he died, and Mary, to the fury of her brother Henry VIII, married his close friend Charles Brandon, Duke of Suffolk, Mary remained in France. She became both lady in waiting to the new queen, Claude, and mistress to Claude's husband, the new French king, François I, who called her his 'hackney' – translation: he liked to ride her.

Mary's reputation proceeded her; she was known as the 'English Mare'. She was clearly a particularly 'friendly' girl with the men at court, so much so that she was relieved of her lady in waiting duties and sent back to England. Ridolfo Pio, the Papal Nuncio in Paris, who had a real axe to grind against the Boleyns (no pun intended) said that François 'knew [Mary] for a very great whore, the most infamous of them all'.

Mary married Sir William Carey, one of Henry's Gentlemen of the Bed Chamber, on 4 February 1520 in Greenwich. The king attended the wedding and clearly liked what he saw in the new bride. Mary soon became his mistress and arguably (Henry never publicly acknowledged either of them) gave birth to two of his illegitimate children, Catherine (born 1524) and Henry (born 1526).

Mary's husband did well out of being cuckolded; he received a number of financial grants and her father, Thomas Boleyn, was made Knight of the Garter, Treasurer of the Household and Viscount Rochford in 1525. Being a royal mistress was clearly nice work if your daughter could get it.

32-year-old William Carey left her in financial dire straits when he died from sweating sickness on 22 June 1528. Anne, who was by now completely in lust with Henry, provided Mary's son Henry Carey with an education by acting as his ward. Later that year, Anne made sure that Henry himself awarded Mary the annuity of £100 (around £32,000 today) that had previously gone to her husband.

Mary was in attendance at her sister Anne's coronation in 1533 and accompanied the king and new queen on their visit to France to see King François in October 1532.

For her second husband, Mary scandalously married for love and far below her social station. In 1534 she married soldier William Stafford. She also turned up at court, pregnant. Her family, including queen Anne, who had not granted their permission, were furious. Mary was subsequently banished from court, her father cut off her allowance and it's safe to say relations between the two sisters were left damaged.

Mary had to write to Thomas Cromwell to proclaim her love for her new husband, beg for financial assistance and make clear that her priorities were personal fulfilment rather than securing the royal crown on her head:

> 'I loved him as well as he did me… I had rather beg my bread with him than to be the greatest queen in Christendom.'

That must have been a smack in the face for Anne. Mary left for Calais to be with her new husband (they would have two children) and it was there that William Stafford would be one of the men sent to meet Anne of Cleves. Mary returned to England in 1539 and died four years later, having successfully removed herself from the chaos at court accompanying her sister's and brother's dramatic fall from grace and subsequent execution. Mary's prior relationship with Henry proved incremental in the downfall of her sister; their intimacy would be cited as a reason for Henry and Anne's marriage being invalid.

Mary's daughter Catherine became lady in waiting to both Anne of Cleves and Catherine Howard. She would marry Sir Francis Knollys and her son Henry Carey was made a Knight of the Garter by Elizabeth I. Mary's descendants include Winston Churchill, Charles Darwin, Diana, Princess of Wales and Elizabeth Bowes-Lyon, the late Queen Mother.

Veronica Franco
(1546–1591)

Sixteenth-century Venetian writer and poet Veronica was one of the *'cortigiana onesta'*, the intellectual courtesans, not to be confused with the lower class *'cortigiana di lume'*, prostitutes who worked the Rialto Bridge and offered only sex.

According to records, there were over 11,654 prostitutes in Venice, which had a population of 100,000. You can do the maths. It was fairly simple to be considered a prostitute in Venice. If you were single and were dating a couple of men, then you were considered one. Or if you were married but separated and still dating a couple of men you were also a prostitute. They'd have a whale of a time attempting to make a clear distinction today.

It was also considered vulgar for a woman to be intelligent, express or even have her own opinion. No change there then. Venetian courtesans were world famous. Beautiful, sensual, sexy, enrobed in colourful and bright clothing, often with ribbons and bare breasts, and high-clogged shoes, it's fair to say they were a tourist attraction as they beckoned to customers from the windows and Venetian bridges.

Thanks to the wealth and generosity of their patrons, their lives would be one of extremely comfortable luxury and financial security. Although it wasn't all plain sailing, as the risk of contracting syphilis from one of their lovers was a very real threat, both to their health and financial security.

Courtesans and aristocratic women actually wore very similar clothing and shoes, but there the resemblance ended. The *'cortigiana onesta'* were well informed, intellectual, articulate and educated - many times more so than the high-bred, more respectable aristocratic women and wives only viewed by society as vehicles of procreation and objects of prestige.

Women like Veronica, who was classically educated alongside her three brothers, could read and write. Politicians and those in power would seek the counsel of these courtesans, ironic considering that women were not allowed to hold any power in the government of the day. The most famous and high-born of Veronica's lovers was Henri III of France, to whom she dedicated two of her sonnets in 'Lettere familiari a diversi' (*Familiar Letters to Various People*). Their relationship is a great example of how a courtesan could, through her affairs with powerful men, effect change and influence in global politics. Veronica embarked on her affair with the king at a pivotal time for her beloved Venice. Its borders threatened by the Ottoman Turks, she persuaded him to provide the republic with ships with which to defend itself.

Her writing was supported by the hugely influential Domenico Venier, a Venetian poet, former senator and the head of Venice's largest literary academy. What set Veronica further apart was that she published two volumes of poetry, the *Terze Rime*, in 1575, followed by *Familiar Letters* in 1580. She played music and was part of an artistic 'salon' of thinkers, philosophers and poets.

Veronica was forced to flee her beloved Venice in 1575 because of the plague and lost most of her money and possessions to looting. She came home in 1577 only to face the Inquisition on charges of witchcraft in 1580 for allegedly bewitching her many happy and loyal noble customers. Her first marriage was likely an arranged one, to a doctor, Paolo Panizza. She had six children from different men, only three of whom survived.

Veronica founded a charity for fellow courtesans whilst also writing letters of caution to friends considering entering their daughters into a life like hers. She died penniless in Venice at the age of 47.

Barbara Palmer, nee Villiers, Duchess of Cleveland, Countess of Castlemaine (17 November 1640-1709)

Barbara was one of England's most famous mistresses, a Restoration era contemporary of Samuel Pepys and Aphra Behn. Pepys references her in his diary, 'I know well enough she is a whore' whilst John Evelyn disparagingly dismissed her as 'a vulgar mannered, arrogant slut'.

Her father William, Viscount Grandison would die at the Battle of Bristol; her mother, the honourable Mary Bayning, remarried his cousin, Charles Villiers, the Earl of Anglesey and sent the young Barbara to country relatives until she was 15.

Recalled to London by an ambitious mother determined she would make a brilliant match, the beautiful, sensual and sexually wilful Barbara soon found her first lover in Philip Stanhope, Earl of Chesterfield.

She was married by the age of 19 to fellow royalist sympathiser Roger Palmer (his father would accurately predict that she would make him utterly miserable); it was a complete mismatch in personalities; Barbara was wild and impulsive, Roger serious and religious. It wasn't to be a long-lasting or faithful marriage; before long she'd be having an affair with Charles, the Prince of Wales.

She would first meet him at The Hague in 1659; entrusted by her Royalist family with the task of bringing him secret papers and money to support him in his endeavours to reclaim the crown; they bonded immediately. On his eventual and triumphant return to London, his first night was spent with her. Her first child, Anne Fitzroy, (the last name indicating royal paternity) was born in 1661. Both Roger and the king claimed paternity.

In 1661, Charles would make Roger 1st Earl Castlemaine, most probably to keep him sweet; it worked for a short time. Roger would formally separate from his wife in 1662 (although they would never actually divorce because he was a strict Catholic), the same year that Catherine of Braganza, Charles's long-suffering wife and the daughter of the king of Portugal, arrived. Charles would bed Barbara on his wedding night, apparently in between his wedding vows, and return to the wedding chamber too 'exhausted' to perform for his new wife.

Barbara was pregnant with the king's second child and was determined to become a Lady of the Bedchamber to the new queen. Catherine had been warned about Barbara and she was furious. Indignantly, she made clear her feelings to Charles. She wouldn't have his mistress so up close and personal in her own household. The king instead presented Barbara to his wife at court; once she realised who she was, the queen fainted. Furious at his wife for not doing what he wanted, he dismissed all her Portuguese ladies, completely alienating her. Barbara had won the first round. Catherine was eventually forced to back down and accept her husband's mistress into her household.

Bishop Burnet described her as 'a woman of great beauty, but more enormously vicious and ravenous, foolish but imperious'. Like Charles's other mistresses, Barbara would be painted by Sir Peter Lely, the official painter to the royal court. Her image would be copied onto engravings and sold en masse to the public who lapped up all the gossip about her. Barbara adored the attention and the privilege. She unashamedly made money selling access to the king and court; she gambled (the king indulgently cleared her debts) she wore extravagant clothes and jewellery; she was given the palace of Nonsuch as a gift but swiftly gutted it, stripping it of its contents and selling them off.

You did not mess with Villiers. She had King Charles II firmly by the short and curlies. She would bear him six children and when he refused to acknowledge the sixth, she threatened to kill the child and made him beg her forgiveness in front of the entire court. His legitimate wife Catherine, however, would prove barren and never provide him with any children.

Barbara wasn't faithful to him. And he wasn't faithful to her. By 1663, his interest would have moved onto the beautiful Frances Stuart; in 1676 Barbara would move to Paris with four of her children and spend the next four years there. She became immensely rich but spent it as quickly as it came in on gambling and jewellery. She was a shrewd political operator.

Barbara had five children with Charles; she may have been Lady Castlemaine, but she was disparagingly referred to as the Royal Whore; diarist John Evelyn called her the 'curse of the nation'. According to Pepys, making reference to a contemporary sexual manual, 'My Lady Castlemaine rules him, who, he says, hath all the tricks of Aretin that are to be practised to give pleasure'.

She is alleged to have taken Charles' own son, the teenaged Duke of Monmouth, as a lover. Other lovers included Charles Hart, (the first lover of Nell Gwynn) and John Churchill, the future Duke of Marlborough.

She died in October 1709 from 'dropsy', or oedema at the age of 68. Legend has it that her ghost haunts Walpole House in Chiswick.

Nell Gwynne
(2 February 1650 - 14 November 1687)

It's a big leap from Drury Lane theatre orange seller, to bawdy comedic Restoration actress, and then onto favourite royal mistress, but Eleanor 'Nell' Gwyn, described by Samuel Pepys as 'pretty, witty Nell', did it with characteristic aplomb. He would also famously refer to her as 'a bold, merry slut'.

Historical sources vary as to whether her story belongs to London, (born in a London back alley, Coal Yard), Hereford's Pipewell Lane (there's still a pub with her name on it in Monkmoor Street) or Oxford, but some facts are constant. Her father Captain Thomas Gwynne was a Welsh soldier, completely ruined by the Civil War, who eventually died in a debtors' prison. Her mother, Madame Ellen Gwynn, kept a brothel in Covent Garden, got drunk and drowned in a pond in Chelsea in July 1679.

Nell is said to have sold 'strong waters' (brandy) to the clientele in her mum's brothel; whether or not she herself worked as a prostitute there is both unclear and unproven. She also variously worked as a herring gutter and possibly a cinder girl and oyster seller.

Together with her older sister Rose, she was signed up as an orange seller in the King's playhouse, called The Theatre - which is now the Theatre Royal in Drury Lane, by former prostitute Mary Meggs or 'Orange Moll'.

It was the early 1660s, Charles II was back on the throne and had thrown open the doors of London's theatres, much to the delight of the public, long sick of the Puritans, Cromwell and Civil War. He put women on the stage (Nell would be one of the first) by legalising the acting profession for them.

It was at The Theatre that Nell caught the eye of actor Charles Hart. They became lovers and with his support, she began acting at around the age of 14 or 15. She was a natural comedic performer. Her first recorded performance was in Dryden's *Indian Emperor* in 1665. The public adored her and her star was on the rise.

Supported by her lover Charles Hart (she would refer to him as Charles I) and later in 1667, Charles Sackville (Nell called him Charles II), Nell was having roles written specifically for her by playwrights including Dryden. She was a member of the Drury Lane company until 1669 and a successful comedic actress in her own right before she encountered the royal Charles and became his mistress in 1668.

It's likely that theirs was a genuine love story – made more authentic by the fact that Nell, unlike Charles's other twelve mistresses, in particular the infamous Lady Castlemaine (Barbara Palmer) didn't actually want anything from him. She wasn't interested in titles or political power.

Regardless, in February 1671, Charles gave her a house at 79 Pall Mall – it belonged to her family until 1693; was demolished in 1866, rebuilt shortly afterwards and is now a Grade II listed building – and an annuity of £4,000. She affectionately referred to the King as her Charles III.

Nell was an epic wit and could hold her own in a politically charged situation; like the time the baying public crowds mistook her for Louise de Keroualle, Duchess of Portsmouth and the hated French Catholic mistress of Charles, 'Pray good people be civil, I am the *Protestant* whore', she exclaimed to their delight.

She would bear Charles, aka the Merry Monarch, two sons. The first, Charles Beauclerk, (born in 1670), would be made Duke of

St. Albans. The second, James, Lord Beauclerk, (born 1671) died at the age of nine.

Legend has it that in 1685, Charles's death bed plea was 'let not poor Nelly starve'. His younger brother and heir, the future James II, fulfilled that promise, paying off Nell's many creditors with Secret Service funds and awarding her a pension of £1,500, worth about £150,000 today.

Following a stroke in March 1687, she was left paralysed down one side of her body. She would suffer a second stroke two months later. She died at her home in 1687 from apoplexy and was buried in the church of St. Martin's-in-the-Fields. The Nell Gwynne pub still stands near London's Strand.

Kate Hackabout (b. Unknown-based on Hogarth's painting, 2 September 1731)

Kate was a London thief, prostitute and the sister of highwayman Francis Hackabout, who following his trial at the Old Bailey, was hanged at Tyburn in 1730 at the age of 28.

Details of her life and death are sketchy at best. Described by the papers of the day, the *Daily Post* and satirical periodical *Grub Street Journal*, (published from January 8, 1730 to 1738) as being:

> 'a very termagant, and a terror, not only to the civil part of the neighbourhood by her frequent fighting, noise, and swearing in the streets in the night-time, but also to other women of her own profession, who presume to pay or pick up men in her district, which is half one side of the way in Bridges-street'.

She was well known in the hundred of Drury, an area by St. Giles in-the-Fields described by the London Spy as:

> '…that ancient and venerable spot …which, I hear, is the property of two or three parishes more. There are reckoned to be one hundred and seven "pleasure-houses" within and about this settlement; and a Roman Catholic priest, who has lodged here many years, assures me that to his knowledge the Societies for the Reformation of Morals have taken as much pains, and expended as large sums to reclaim this new Sodom, as would have fitted out a force sufficient to have conquered the Spanish West Indies.'

Following a raid of houses of disrepute on Bridges Street on 3 August 1730, Kate was tried and sentenced to hard labour at Bridewell prison by Westminster magistrate Sir John Gonson (who also appears in Hogarth's series) as punishment for keeping a disorderly or bawdy house. Following that, she frustratingly disappears from history altogether.

Together with fellow prostitute Mary Collins, she is said to have inspired the Georgian character Moll Hackabout in Hogarth's first plate in the 1731 Harlot's Progress series of six paintings, depicting the fall from grace into prostitution and degradation of an innocent upon her arrival in the capital and subsequent meeting with procuress Elizabeth 'Mother' Needham. Moll, clearly a common name at the time for women of dubious reputation, is undoubtedly a mix of both real and imagined historical characters.

Analysing her story further, the word 'hack' from her last name 'Hackabout' was slang for 'harlot' as it links to a hackney carriage, which any could and many did, ride in. A commentary on the precarious position many country women found themselves in upon their arrival in London, it's also suggested that Moll is inspired by Daniel Defoe's *Moll Flanders*, which was published in 1722:

> 'The Fortunes and Misfortunes of the Famous Moll Flanders Who was born in Newgate, and during a life of continu'd Variety for Threescore Years, besides her Childhood, was Twelve Years a Whore, five times a Wife (whereof once to her brother) Twelve Years a Thief, Eight Years a Transported Felon in Virginia, at last grew Rich, liv'd Honest and died a Penitent.'

In turn, Moll Flanders is based on the life of criminal Elizabeth Adkins (1696-1747) aka Moll King, who Defoe met in Newgate Prison.

Madame/Marquise de Pompadour (c. December 1721-15 April 1764)

Pompadour was a powerful and influential courtesan at the sumptuous court of Louis XV of France. At the French king's side for two decades, she began life in Paris in 1721 as the rather more ordinary-sounding Jeanne-Antoinette Poisson.

Her father, François Poisson, worked for wealthy financiers. However, it's rumoured that her real biological father was one of her mother's lovers, possibly tax collector Charles Le Normant de Tournehem, who paid for Jeanne-Antoinette's education, during the time shortly after her birth that Francois, desperate to escape a death sentence for fraud, fled France.

Jeanne's mother, the great beauty Madeleine de La Motte, groomed her for greatness. She was given an education at an Ursuline convent and endured rigorous elocution lessons from the very best that Parisian opera and theatre had to offer. She also received a thorough political and economic education at the exclusive men's Club de l'Entresol.

In 1741, at the age of 20, she was married off to Tournehem's nephew and moved into an impressive estate at Etoiles; the couple would have two children, a son who died young and a daughter, Alexandrine, nicknamed 'Fanfan'. Jeanne soon gained a reputation for her intellectual salons, which attracted artists, philosophers and writers including Voltaire.

The king and Jeanne are said to have met at a fancy dress party, the Clipped Yew Tree Ball in 1745, held to celebrate the marriage of the dauphin Louis-Ferdinand. Jeanne came as a shepherdess and the king dressed as a tree. In the eighteenth century version of the 'walk of shame', her carriage was spotted outside his residence the following morning. The game was on.

Portrait of Madame de Pompadour, by Charles Nicolas Cochin II, ca. 1745.

At the age of 23, she became the king's mistress, securing apartments at Versailles, connected to his by a secret staircase. The king was married to Marie Leszczynska, with whom he would have ten children. Jeanne, meanwhile, swiftly separated from her husband and organised for her young daughter, Alexandrine, to be taken off her hands. Later that year, the king would award Jeanne the estates of Pompadour and create her a Marquise, officially presenting her at court in September 1745. It took a year for her to be elevated to position of Maitresse en Titre - chief mistress.

Being the mistress to the king was a physically and emotionally exhausting, full-time job. The Pompadour wore herself out entertaining him. Her entire life, her very being, was subjugated to his every whim, amusement, entertainment and happiness. She didn't actually enjoy the sexual part of the relationship (which lasted around five years) and ate food which was reputed to encourage sexual passion, including 'vanilla, celery and truffles', in a bid to boost her flagging libido.

The king became step father to FanFan, who died just before her tenth birthday. Whilst Pompadour put on a masterful front, (her existence at the centre of the king's universe relied on her acting happy and never giving him cause for any emotion that wasn't positive), it's likely she never recovered from the devastating loss.

Eventually, the king's relationship with Pompadour became platonic and she organised alternative sexual partners for him, careful never to choose anyone who would impact on her control over him. Madame meanwhile, reinvented herself as a major domo patron of artists including Francois Boucher. Ironically, you could say she took on the traditional role of a royal wife – all the perks and privilege without actually having to sleep with him.

She was pivotal in commissioning the creation of the now legendary Sevres porcelain factory, was a major fan and proponent of the Rococo style and persuaded the king to create the Petit Trianon which would become infamous under the doomed Marie Antoinette.

She was an incredible one-woman intellectual dynamo, encouraging the creation and publication of the first two volumes of

Diderot and d'Alembert's *Encyclopaedia* and becoming a patron to writers, including her old friend Voltaire, who through her influence, became the royal court's historiographer. She had an incredible and substantial private library comprising some 3,500 volumes.

At 42 years old, her body worn out from numerous miscarriages, a fight with tuberculosis and the rigours of palace and political life, she died at Versailles on Easter Sunday 1764. She was buried next to her daughter FanFan.

Madame du Barry
(19 August 1743 - 8 December 1793)

Out with the old, in with the new. Madame Pompadour was dead. And moving in to take her place was Jeanne Becu, the last 'maitresse en titre' of French King Louis XV, who moved into Versailles in 1768. They met in 1768; at this point, Louis was nearly sixty years old and Jeanne in her twenties. The illegitimate daughter of low-class parents, she started life with a convent education, before progressing to assistant in a Parisian fashion house. Her life as a

mistress began with arms contractor and nobleman Jean du Barry; her beauty and his links to society meant that it wasn't long before she caught the eye of the king.

Louis lost no time in legitimatising his latest paramour. Ridiculous logic as it sounds, she couldn't be his official mistress unless she was married to a noble. Thus, the Count Guillaume du Barry, Jean's brother, was persuaded to marry Jeanne; he was then paid off to disappear and the newly enobled Jeanne du Barry was presented at court in April 1769. Fait accompli. Job done.

Jeanne had a notoriously fractious relationship with Marie Antoinette, who first caught a glimpse of her on the eve of her own wedding to the dauphin, at a dinner at the castle of La Muette. When an embarrassed courtier explained of Madame du Barry that 'the lady was there to give pleasure to the king', the naïve Antoinette replied, 'Oh, then I shall be her rival, because I too wish to give pleasure to the king.'

When she finally realised the role du Barry played both at court and in the king's boudoir, Marie, brought up in a more chaste and Catholic court, was morally horrified. Egged on by the king's own sisters, she refused to publicly acknowledge du Barry. That is, until New Year's Day 1772 when, under huge pressure from both her mother, Empress Maria Theresa and the Austrian ambassador, and likely doing it through gritted teeth, the Dauphine managed to utter, if not directly to Madame du Barry, then somewhere in her person's vicinity, 'There are a lot of people today at Versailles'.

Before the onset of the Revolution, du Barry spent her days living very comfortably at her chateau in Louveciennes, gifted to her by the king, and was a generous art patron. She commissioned pieces from painters Fragonard and Vien, as well as joiner Delanois and cabinet maker Leleu, and was a personal friend of Voltaire.

Following the king's death in May 1774, she was banished by the new king, Louis XVI, forced out of Versailles and sent to a convent.

Denounced as a counter-revolutionary, (she had made several trips to London, probably to financially support desperate French emigres) she lost her head to the guillotine in October 1793, shrieking and screaming for mercy all the way. Her last words, directed to her executioner, were, 'Encore un moment, monsieur le bourreau, un petit moment.' ('One moment more, executioner, one little moment.')

Grace Dalrymple (c. 1754 - 1823)

A spy and courtesan who survived divorce and the French Revolution, Grace was born in Scotland, probably Edinburgh, around 1754. Her father was lawyer Hugh (Hew) Dalrymple, Governor General of Grenada in the Caribbean; her mother Grizel (Scottish version of Grace) died in 1767.

Grace was educated in a French convent and married off in October 1771 or October 1772 to Dr. John Eliot, a Scottish doctor twice his new bride's age. He would have affairs and a mistress; it was expected that Grace would just accept it. What wasn't acceptable to her husband was Grace herself having affairs, which she did with 'player' Arthur Annesley, eighth Viscount Valentia, even making the gossip columns in 1774 and 1775 when she ran away with him. Her husband was likely apopletic at the humiliation. He filed for divorce in 1774.

Grace gave birth to a son, who died young and she was divorced via a Criminal Conversation case. With no options left to her, she became a courtesan who would be painted by Gainsborough and Reynolds.

The Prince of Wales (later George IV) fell for her after glimpsing her miniature; their affair resulted in a (not publicly acknowledged) daughter, Georgiana Augusta Frederica, born 30 March 1782. Her other lovers included the Fourth Earl of Cholmondeley and Louis Philippe II, the French Duc d'Orleans, (cousin to the doomed Louis XVI, he'd vote for the King's death and himself be executed on 6 November 1793).

She smuggled letters to and from England and France during the French Revolution, a time of immense danger for her. After one particularly terrifying incident, as she attempted to flee Paris for her country home in Meudon, she wrote:

'[I was] in fear every minute of meeting the patrole or murderers, till I got to the bottom of the steep hill which leads up to the Château of Meudon, my house being on the top of the hill. I had never looked back: my heart beat hard. I thought every moment that I was followed. About the middle of the hill I saw a man coming towards me, and was so much terrified that I dropped down among the vines which border the hill, quite losing my senses. On my recovery I neither heard nor saw anybody. Perhaps it was some poor wretch making his escape, who was as much alarmed as I was. I was then not very far from my own house, and with great pain I reached it, but so much fatigued and agitated that they were obliged to undress and put me to bed almost senseless. My feet were covered with blood, having no soles to my shoes or stockings. My shoes were thin white silk, and the road is very stony.'

She was even tasked with a parcel from Marie Antoinette in an attempt, (ultimately doomed), to get the royal family out of the country.

She was questioned many times by Revolutionary guards, the Comité de Surveillance and spent time in prison with Josephine de Beauharnais, the future wife of Napoleon and infamous Empress Josephine. Grace was ultimately saved by Robespierre himself, who was guillotined before her execution order could be fulfilled.

Once back in England, she wrote her memoirs, *Journal of My Life During the French Revolution*. They were never meant to be published but when they were, in 1859 by her granddaughter, they were heavily edited.

She died in Ville d'Avray, Paris on 15 May 1823.

Harriette Wilson
(22 February 1786 - 10 March 1845)

'Having no other power or public voice, the betrayed
woman reaches for her pen.'
Harriette Wilson

'The courtesan was expected to provide all the shades
of companionship without the oppressive limitations
and implications of marriage. She offered not only the
bed but the sofa, the dinner-table and the salon – all
save the nursery and the kitchen.'
Lesley Blanch, 'Harriette
Wilson's Memoirs' (Century, 1985)

Harriette was an accomplished Regency courtesan, contemporary
and correspondent of Byron (who would gift her the sum of one
thousand francs), Jane Austen, and notable courtesans of the time
including Elizabeth Armistead, (who went on to marry politician
Charles James Fox).

Harriette was the daughter of Swiss clock maker John James
Dubochet and his wife Amelia Cook. Born in Mayfair, one of fifteen
children (nine of whom survived) she failed twice in her attempts to
undertake employment as a governess, one of the very few employment
opportunities open to women at the time. The second time she returned
home, her father hit her. Eager to escape life there, where she and her
sisters would mend stockings for a living, she went to Brighton and
became mistress to William, Earl of Craven at the age of 15. She wrote
disparagingly of his practice of wearing a night cap to bed:

'Surely ... all men do not wear those shocking
nightcaps; else all women's illusions had been
destroyed on the first night of their marriage.'

She soon entered London's high society as a hugely successful courtesan, reigning supreme from her opera box, using her literary talent, intelligence and keen wit to win the minds, hearts and purses of paramours and protectors, spending lavishly and employing a veritable retinue of staff including a housekeeper, coach, cook and footman. Writing her memoirs was, as she freely admitted, 'a desperate effort to live by my wits', when in her thirties, her looks fading and her admirers proving fickle, she'd been promised an annual living from the Duke of Beaufort in exchange for staying away from his heir, the Marquis of Worcester. He reneged on the deal, leaving her penniless. Quite a few of them did the same – and moved on from her to one of the three sisters, Amy, Sophia and Fanny, who all became courtesans. Sophia became the mistress of Lord Deerhurst aged 13, whilst Amy would have a son by Harriette's former lover, the Duke of Argyll.

Harriette was completely against marriage, the example of her parents' own influencing her to write:

> '... my dear mother's marriage had proved to me so forcibly the miseries of two people of contrary opinions and character torturing each other to the end of their natural lives, that, before I was ten years old, I decided in my own mind to live free as air from any restraint but that of my own conscience.'

She fell in love with Lord Ponsonby, who allegedly broke her heart by dumping her after three years for her much younger sister Sophia, who would go on to marry well, becoming Lady Berwick at the age of 17.

Harriette grew older, moved to Paris to retire and, to help him escape debtors' prison, married William Henry Rochfort, a doubtful, shadowy figure and former soldier in South America, who financially drained her whilst simultaneously and dubiously claiming Irish aristocratic heritage. They lived at 111 rue du Faubourg St Honoré.

Meanwhile, her former lovers broke their previous passionate promises to provide for her financially. Facing financial ruin, she decided to write her memoirs, which were published in nine sensational and hugely anticipated instalments, between February and August 1825. It's reported that barricades had to be used to control the mob desperate to get their hands on the first episode. At the end of each instalment, she wrote a teaser, suggesting who would be named in the next excerpt; it offered those threatened with the ignominy of being revealed the opportunity to pay their way out it. Just think of the number of stories we are the poorer for, due to their lack of inclusion.

Sir Walter Scott wrote:

> 'The gay world has been kept in hot water lately by the impudent publication of the celebrated Harriot Wilson, who lived with half the gay world at hack and manger, and now obliges such as will not pay hush money with a history of whatever she knows or invents about them.'

Harriette actually wrote a letter to each of her many lovers, who included a large proportion of the political Establishment, including the Duke of Wellington, the Honourable Frederick Lamb (son of Lord Melbourne), the Earl of Craven (her first lover) the Marquess of Worcester and the Duke of Argyll, offering to keep them out of the book, for £200 in total or £20 a year.

The Duke of Wellington's letter, sent from Harriette's publisher John Stockdale, read:

> 'My Lord Duke, in Harriette Wilson's Memoirs, which I am about to publish, are various anecdotes of Your

Grace which it would be most desirable to withhold, at least such is my opinion. I have stopped the Press for the moment, but as the publication will take place next week, little delay can necessarily take place.'

Legend has it that a furious Wellington allegedly wrote, 'Publish, and be damned' on his letter. The veracity of this claim aside, she did publish and the depictions of the great Wellington, compared to a rat-catcher in the accompanying cartoons, weren't flattering. Half the aristocracy were named in the book, which had 31 editions in its first year, with versions made available across Europe to the delight of the scandal-loving readers of France and Germany.

Harriette possessed incriminating letters from George IV's lover and he was willing to 'do anything to suppress what Harriette had to reveal of [his mistress] Lady Conyngham'. If you paid up, she'd be complimentary in her writings. Blackmail it was, but it's hard not to admire her sheer chutzpah and refusal to play the victim. How else was she to fend for herself financially, having been promised security and then abandoned? 'I never attempted to expose them,' Harriette wrote, 'till all my civil, humble, and abject prayers and protestations had failed to wring from their impenetrable hearts one single paltry hundred a year.' Her publisher John Joseph Stockdale was sent to prison for extortion.

Harriette died in Paris; by the end of her life she was a convert to Catholicism and a figure of obscurity.

Esther Lachmann aka La Païva
(1819-84)

Esther Pauline Lachmann, later known as the Countess Henkel von Donnersmarck, was said to be a nasty piece of work.

What she lacked in traditional beauty, she more than made up for in ruthless ambition. The Russian daughter of Jewish Polish and German parents, she slept her way from the streets of a Moscow ghetto to the upper echelons of 19th century Parisian society as a Countess during the time of The French Second Republic.

She would be accused of being a German spy and counted Emperor Napoleon III as just one of her many admirers. She first got married in 1836, at the age of 17, to a tailor who had tuberculosis.

Soon after, she left him, and the son she bore, for Paris to seek her fortune and changed her name to Therese.

Therese started off as a lowly sex worker and spent three years meticulously, almost obsessively, preparing for her grand assault on high society. She had a passionate, almost obsessive belief in the power of complete self-will. In 1841 at the age of 22, she set out for Ems, a spa town in Prussia, her bags packed with fake jewellery and borrowed evening wear.

It didn't take her long to capture the affections and pampered patronage of wealthy pianist Henri Herz. He bestowed upon her an apartment, clothes and jewels. She bankrupted him a few years later, partially through her sumptuous and popular salon, which was graced by the presence of luminaries including composer Richard Wagner and journalist Émile de Girardin. Henri left for America and his family threw Therese out of the house.

She left for London, where she met, swiftly secured and married the Portuguese marquis Albino Francesco Araújo de Païva. The relationship was short lived, probably about as long as it took her to plough through his fortune. Having bled him dry and having no further use for him, she said:

> 'You wanted to sleep with me, and you've done so, by making me your wife. You have given me your name, I acquitted myself last night. I have behaved like an honest woman, I wanted a position, and I've got it, but all you have is a prostitute for a wife. You can't take me anywhere, and you can't introduce me to anyone. We must therefore separate. You go back to Portugal. I shall stay here with your name, and remain a whore.'

He duly returned to Lisbon and committed suicide.

She was now a courtesan with a noble title under her belt. And next up for conquest was the ridiculously wealthy Count Henckel von Donnersmarck, one of the richest men in Europe. She married him in 1871. He bankrolled the building of The Hôtel de la Païva; situated at 25 Champs Elysees, it was built between 1856 and 1866 and its extravagances included erotic parties, a solid yellow onyx staircase and marble bathtubs with jewelled taps, regularly filled with champagne or milk. It still stands, today housing the Travellers Club, which ironically, considering it was built by a woman, only allowed women entrance relatively recently.

Her detractors said of her:

> 'On the surface, the face is that of a courtesan who will not be too old for her profession when she is a hundred

years old, but underneath, another face is visible from time to time, the terrible face of a painted corpse.'

She died at the count's country chateau in Poland in 1884. He was so devastated that he placed her body in embalming fluid and kept it in the attic. He would weep over it each night and its discovery proved one hell of a shock for his next wife.

La Barucci (Giulia Beneni) 1837[?]-70/1)

Giulia clearly believed in the phrase 'Italians do it better' and made it her personal mantra. She also referred to herself as 'The Greatest Whore in the World', the real life Venus de Milo and lived in a sumptuous mansion on the Champs Elysees, said to have a luxurious staircase of white carpet and banisters covered in velvet.

She had a carefree air that captivated men – including the army general who was so desperate to sleep with her that he obeyed her instruction to appear before her, outside her house at 124 Boulevarde Malesherbes, at the head of his troops, on horseback, naked.

In 1867, she was invited to meet Albert Edward (Bertie), the Prince of Wales (the future Edward VII); She was given protocol advice and told to be on time. She wasn't. She kept him waiting for nearly an hour, then on finally meeting him, dropped her clothes, showing him 'the white rotundities of her callipygian charms'. When chastised for her impertinence, she retorted: 'What, did you not tell me to behave properly to His Royal Highness? I showed him the best I have, and it was free!'

Clearly her approach worked a treat as the Prince became her lover, and following her death, was blackmailed by Giulia's brother to the tune of 6,000 Francs to prevent their correspondence becoming public.

Incidentally, Bertie had a reputation as a frequenter of the Parisian brothels; so much so that an 'armchair of love' was commissioned by him for personal use in a private room at the brothel Le Chabanais. It was designed to allow Bertie to 'entertain' two women at the same time. The mind boggles.

A contemporary (and rival) of Victorian courtesans Cora Pearl (who met Prince Edward wearing only a string of pearls and a piece of parsley) and La Paiva, she worked out of Paris in an opulent mansion on the Champs Elysses, and had a jewellery cabinet filled with priceless gems which she loved to show off to visitors; she also kept her men's calling cards in a china bowl by her fireplace – by all accounts, it was one hell of a collection, featuring the names of the majority of high society.